BLES

Arranged for Private Prayer

●

With a Short Helpful Meditation
Before Each Novena

By

REV. LAWRENCE G. LOVASIK, S.V.D.
Divine Word Missionary

Illustrated in Color

CATHOLIC BOOK PUBLISHING CO.
New Jersey

NIHIL OBSTAT: James M. Cafone, M.A., S.T.D.
Censor Librorum

IMPRIMATUR: ✠ Most Rev. John J. Myers, D.D., S.T.D.
Archbishop of Newark

ABBREVIATIONS OF THE BOOKS OF THE BIBLE

Acts—Acts of the Apostles	Jb—Job	Nm—Numbers
Am—Amos	Jdt—Judith	Ob—Obadiah
Bar—Baruch	Jer—Jeremiah	Phil—Philippians
1 Chr—1 Chronicles	Jgs—Judges	Phlm—Philemon
2 Chr—2 Chronicles	Jl—Joel	Prv—Proverbs
Col—Colossians	Jn—John	Ps(s)—Psalms
1 Cor—1 Corinthians	1 Jn—1 John	1 Pt—1 Peter
2 Cor—2 Corinthians	2 Jn—2 John	2 Pt—2 Peter
Dn—Daniel	3 Jn—3 John	Rom—Romans
Dt—Deuteronomy	Jon—Jonah	Ru—Ruth
Eccl—Ecclesiastes	Jos—Joshua	Rv—Revelation
Eph—Ephesians	Jude—Jude	Sir—Sirach
Est—Esther	1 Kgs—1 Kings	1 Sm—1 Samuel
Ex—Exodus	2 Kgs—2 Kings	2 Sm—2 Samuel
Ez—Ezekiel	Lam—Lamentations	Song—Song of Songs
Ezr—Ezra	Lk—Luke	Tb—Tobit
Gal—Galatians	Lv—Leviticus	1 Thes—1 Thessalonians
Gn—Genesis	Mal—Malachi	2 Thes—2 Thessalonians
Hb—Habakkuk	1 Mc—1 Maccabees	Ti—Titus
Heb—Hebrews	2 Mc—2 Maccabees	1 Tm—1 Timothy
Hg—Haggai	Mi—Micah	2 Tm—2 Timothy
Hos—Hosea	Mk—Mark	Wis—Wisdom
Is—Isaiah	Mt—Matthew	Zec—Zechariah
Jas—James	Na—Nahum	Zep—Zephaniah
	Neh—Nehemiah	

(T-62)

FOREWORD

A NOVENA means nine days of public or private prayer for some special occasion or intention. Its origin goes back to the nine days that the disciples and Mary spent together in prayer between Ascension and Pentecost Sunday. Over the centuries many novenas have been highly indulgenced by the Church.

To make a novena means to persevere in prayer asking for some favor over a period of nine days in succession or nine weeks. It means fulfilling our Lord's teaching that we must continue praying and never lose confidence. This confidence is based on our Lord's words: "Ask and you will receive; seek and you will find; knock and it will be opened to you. For whoever asks receives; whoever seeks finds; whoever knocks is admitted" (Lk 11:9-10).

The Eucharist is the Sacrament which contains the true Body and Blood of Jesus Christ, together with His Soul and Divinity, the entire living and glorified Christ, under the appearances of bread and wine.

There are three different aspects or phases of the Eucharist. The first is called the Real Presence of Christ on the altar while there remains a consecrated Host in the tabernacle. The second phase of the Eucharist is the Sacrifice of the Mass, and the third is Holy Communion.

The Eucharist is reserved in our churches to be a powerful help to prayer and the service of others. Reservation of the Blessed Sacrament means that at the end of Communion the remaining Consecrated Bread is placed in the tabernacle and reverently reserved. The Eucharist reserved is a continuing sign of our Lord's real presence among His people and spiritual food for the sick and dying.

The Novena in honor of the Sacrament of the Holy Eucharist can be made many times during the Liturgical Year to deepen our faith in this great mystery of love, the center of all Sacramental life of the Church.

Try to talk with God during your novena. Absolute sincerity is most important. And as you grow in daily reflection and prayer, you will find yourself talking to God with much the same ease as you would converse with a close friend.

Use your own words in this simple, intimate chat with God, and they will gradually become your own personal, individual way of prayer. You will find that the Holy Spirit is enlightening your mind and strengthening your will to do God's Will.

Father Lawrence G. Lovasik, S.V.D.

CONTENTS

HEART-TALK
ON THE
HOLY SACRIFICE OF THE MASS

"Do this in remembrance of Me."

A MOST WORTHY SACRIFICE

JESUS, before You came upon earth, the people of the Old Testament offered sacrifices to God in order to honor Him as their Creator and Master. All their victims of sacrifice were but weak figures of the true Victim Who offered Himself on Calvary. You are that Victim, O Jesus. You alone are able to offer the only Sacrifice worthy of God because You are a Divine Person, God's own Son. As the God-Man You are the Divine High Priest and Mediator between God and men.

The Sacrifices of animals and the fruits of the earth could not satisfy God. Your Sacrifice on the Cross, however, was most pleasing to Him. It made us friends of God and merited every heavenly blessing for us. Through it God was perfectly adored, and due thanks were paid to Him for all that He had done for men. Our sins were atoned for and pardoned.

OUR SACRIFICE

JESUS, in order that the merits of Your Sacrifice on Calvary might be applied to every soul of every time, You willed that it should be renewed upon the altar; therefore You instituted the Sacrifice of the Mass at the Last Supper. By Your words; "Do this in remembrance of Me," You gave Your Apostles and their successors not only the power to consecrate but the command, also, to do what You Yourself had done at the Last Supper. You made them priests that they might carry on until the end of time the Sacrifice of our Redemption in Your Church on earth.

Your Sacrifice did not cease when You were taken down from the Cross; You appear daily on our altars as the Eternal High Priest and Victim, continuing Your first and only offering. The altar is another Calvary; for that which is offered and given upon the altar is the Body that was broken for me, the Blood that was shed for my salvation. On the Cross You were offered in a bloody manner, while in the Sacrifice of the Mass You are offered in an unbloody manner.

The Last Supper, the Sacrifice of the Cross, and Holy Mass are *one and the same Sacrifice,* and You are the only Victim. At the Last Supper You made one offering of Yourself to Your Heavenly Father. It was carried out and completed on the Cross and is continued at Mass. On Calvary You redeemed us and merited graces for us. Our souls receive these graces at Holy Mass.

A REMEMBRANCE AND A SACRIFICE

JESUS, I believe that the Mass is a *remembrance* of Your Passion and Death, for You said at the Last Supper, "Do this in remembrance of Me." Jesus, help me to remember Pope John Paul's words: "The Eucharistic Sacrifice includes not only the Mystery of [Your] Passion and Death but also the Mystery of the Resurrection which crowned [Your] Sacrifice. It is as the living and Risen one that [You] can become in the Eucharist the 'Bread of Life' (Jn 6:35, 48), the 'Living Bread' (Jn 6:51)."

No Mass is celebrated, no Communion received without my being enabled to remember that You delivered Yourself up to death for the redemption of the world. Your painful death on the Cross is represented at Mass by the double Consecration of the bread and the wine. I look upon the Sacred Host lying on the altar, separated from the chalice; and I think of the slow bleeding by which Your Blood was separated from Your Body on the Cross. I wish to attend Mass often, in order that I may in this way show my gratitude to You for having died on the Cross out of love for me.

I believe that Holy Mass is also a true *sacrifice*—the Sacrifice of Calvary offered again, no more in a bloody manner, but in an unbloody manner under the appearances of bread and wine. After the Consecration You become present on the altar as the Priest and Victim of Calvary, and through the hands of the priest You offer Yourself again to Your Father with all the acts of adoration, abandonment and love which You once offered to Him on the Cross. Therefore I desire to offer You to Your Father as the greatest gift that alone is worthy of God: to adore Him as my Creator, to thank Him as my greatest Benefactor, to make atonement for all my sins against Him, and to pray for all that I need in body and soul.

God of the Eucharist, You died for me! How can I ever forget You when Mass brings Calvary so close to me? How can this most generous and entire sacrifice of Yourself fail to impress me when at Mass I see You laid on the altar, the Victim of Calvary? Your Sacrifice of love is too beautiful to be forgotten. I want to remember You. I want to offer You as a Sacrifice to God, and to offer myself together with You—at Mass.

THE GREATEST GIFT

JESUS, help me to realize that the Mass *is the greatest gift of God to man, and man's greatest gift to God*—the central act of Christian worship. I can do nothing better to honor God the Father than to unite myself with Your own Sacrifice, for never was He worshiped in a manner deserving of His Majesty until You humbly made Yourself a Victim on Calvary. As wayward children we have dishonored our Heavenly Father by sin, but as our Redeemer You have atoned for this infinite offense by Your death on the Cross.

God wanted Your Sacrifice to be the only sacrifice that should be offered up throughout all ages everywhere in the world. By accepting the Sacrifice of the Cross, He also accepted the Sacrifice of the Mass, which is a continuation of Your Sacrifice on the Cross.

Jesus, I believe that Holy Mass is the most perfect homage which can be offered to God; that one single Mass gives more glory to God than He could receive from the combined homage of all the Angels and Saints throughout eternity. I, a poor creature, rejoice at the thought that each day I can offer to God an act of homage that is worthy of His Majesty, an act of thanksgiving that is equal to the greatness of the benefits I have received from Him, an act of atonement that can fully make up for my terrible offenses against my Heavenly Father, a prayer for assistance that God cannot refuse. I firmly believe that Holy Mass means all this to me because at Mass I offer to my Heavenly Father His own Son, the Victim of Calvary.

I thank You, dear Lord, for having entrusted this great treasure to the Catholic Church. Help us all to appreciate its infinite value as far as we are able.

A SCHOOL OF SUFFERING

JESUS, my life is full of trials and pain, but in Your Divine compassion You have made Holy Mass a school of suffering where I can learn to make my crosses a means to greater holiness and merit. I know that during Mass You offer Yourself, though in an unbloody manner, to Your Father just as You did on the Cross, in the same spirit of love and resignation to His Divine Will, because You are present in the Sacred Host as the Victim of Calvary. Even in heaven You are still our Victim and Mediator, always interceding for us.

But it is then only that You are really my Victim when I offer myself with You on the altar, in order to share by my generosity and sacrifice in Your life of immolation. I am a member of the Church, Your spiritual Body, and therefore I cannot remain inactive when, as the Head of the Body, You are sacrificing Yourself. For this reason I unite all the work, pains and disappointments of life with Your Sacrifice at Holy Mass, in that spirit of loving resignation and devoted obedience in which You make Your offering. I willingly accept all that God may see fit to send me, the pleasant and the unpleasant, joy or sorrow.

Divine Victim of the Altar, give my heart sentiments like Your own that I may become a worthy co-victim with You. Supply what is wanting to my spirit of sacrifice and generosity. I trust that the works and sufferings of my life, though poor in themselves, will become most precious in God's sight because they are one with Your Divine Sacrifice at Mass.

HIS HEART'S DEAREST GIFT

JESUS, I believe that the holy Sacrifice of the Mass, in which You offer Yourself to God through Your Church, is the greatest act the world has ever seen, for it is Your infinite Sacrifice of Calvary renewed on the altar in an unbloody manner. Through it You give honor and glory to God and apply the fruits of Your Passion and Death to our souls.

May Your Sacrifice on the altar draw all men to Your Most Sacred Heart, as You once said: "And I, if I be lifted up from the earth will draw all things to Myself." At Mass You are again lifted up as You were on Calvary. How touchingly You seem to invite souls and to plead with all the loving eloquence of Your Sacred Heart, "Come to Me, all you who labor and are burdened, and I will give you rest. Friend, come to My Sacrifice! Offer Me to My Heavenly Father. Offer yourself as a sacrifice together with Me. In the Mass I will give you all: forgiveness, grace, joy, peace, for I will give you Myself. My Heart's dearest gift to you is *the Mass.*"

God of the Eucharist, how generous You are! Little do I realize what Holy Mass really means for me. Would that I had millions of hearts to offer to You in gratitude for this Treasure of infinite worth! You have given me all in Your

Sacrifice. Behold, I want to give You all. I offer myself to You entirely, all that I am and have, that I may become one with You on the altar as co-victim—one sacrifice to God with You—at Mass. Amen.

NOVENA
IN HONOR OF THE
HOLY EUCHARIST

MEDITATION

THE Eucharist is the Sacrament which contains the true Body and Blood of Jesus Christ, together with His Soul and Divinity, the entire living and glorified Christ, under the appearances of bread and wine.

The Council of Trent clearly defines the truth that is the very foundation of all Christ-life and worship: "In the Most Holy Sacrament of the Eucharist there is contained truly, really, and substantially, the Body and Blood of our Lord Jesus Christ, together with His Soul and Divinity, indeed the whole Christ."

As Catholics we believe that Jesus Christ remains personally present on the altar as long as there is a consecrated Host in the tabernacle. He is the same Jesus Christ, true God and true Man, Who walked the streets of Galilee and Judea. We believe that He actually comes as our personal guest every time we receive Holy Communion.

The Eucharist is one of the seven Sacraments instituted by Christ to give us a share in the life of God. It is the greatest of all seven Sacraments since It contains Christ Himself, the Divine Author of the Sacraments.

There are three different aspects or phases of the Eucharist. The first is called the Real Presence of Christ on the altar while there remains a consecrated Host in the tabernacle. The second phase of the Eucharist is the Sacrifice of the Mass, and the third is Holy Communion.

The word "Eucharist," from the Greek, means "Thanksgiving." It is applied to this Sacrament because our Lord gave thanks to His Father when He instituted It, and also because the Holy Sacrifice of the Mass is the best means of expressing our thanks to God for His favors.

The Holy Eucharist is the very center of Catholic worship, the heart of Catholic life. Because the Church believes that the Son of God is truly present in the Blessed Sacrament, she erects beautiful churches and adorns them richly.

The Sacrifice of the Mass is not only a ritual which reminds us of the sacrifice of Calvary. In it, through the ministry of priests, Christ continues till the end of time the sacrifice of the Cross in an unbloody manner.

The Eucharist is also a meal which reminds us of the Last Supper, celebrates our unity together in Christ, and already now makes present the Messianic banquet of the Kingdom of heaven.

In the Eucharist Jesus nourishes Christians with His own Self, the Bread of Life, so that they may become a people more pleasing to God and filled with greater love of God and neighbor.

The Novena in honor of the Sacrament of the Holy Eucharist can be made many times during the Liturgical Year to deepen our faith in this great mystery of love, the center of all Sacramental life of the Church.

THE WORD OF GOD

"I am the Bread of life. Your ancestors ate the manna in the wilderness, and yet they died. This is the Bread that comes down from heaven so that one may eat it and never die. I Myself am the living Bread come down from heaven. Whoever eats this Bread will live forever; and the Bread I will give is My Flesh, for the life of the world. . . .

"Unless you eat the Flesh of the Son of Man and drink His Blood, you do not have life within you. Whoever eats My Flesh and drinks My Blood has eternal life, and I will raise him up on the last day. For My Flesh is real food and My Blood is real drink.

"Whoever eats My Flesh and drinks My Blood dwells in Me, and I in him. Just as the living Father sent Me and I have life because of the Father, so whoever eats Me will have life because of Me."   —Jn 6:48-57

"Jesus took bread, and after He had pronounced the blessing, He broke it and gave it to His disciples, saying, 'Take this and eat; this is My Body.' Then He took a cup, and after offering thanks He gave it to them, saying, 'Drink from this, all of you. For this is My Blood of the Covenant, which will be shed on behalf of many for the forgiveness of sins.' "   —Mt 26:26-28

"Do this in remembrance of Me."   —Lk 22:19

NOVENA PRAYERS

Novena Prayer

I THANK You, Jesus, my Divine Redeemer, for coming upon the earth for our sake, and for instituting the adorable Sacrament of the Holy Eucharist in order to remain with us until the end of the world. I thank You for hiding beneath the Eucharistic species Your infinite majesty and beauty, which Your Angels delight to behold, so that I might have courage to approach the throne of Your mercy.

I thank You, most loving Jesus, for having made Yourself my food, and for uniting me to Yourself with so much love in this wonderful Sacrament that I may live in You.

I thank You, my Jesus, for giving Yourself to me in this Blessed Sacrament, and so enriching it with the treasures of Your love that You have no greater gift to give me. I thank You not only for becoming my food but also for offering Yourself as a continual Sacrifice to Your Eternal Father for my salvation.

I thank You, Divine Priest, for offering Yourself as a Sacrifice daily upon our altars in adoration and homage to the Most Blessed Trinity, and for making amends for our poor and miserable adorations. I thank You for renewing in this daily Sacrifice the actual Sacrifice of the Cross offered on Calvary, in which You satisfy Divine justice for us poor sinners.

I thank You, dear Jesus, for having become the priceless Victim to merit for me the fullness of heavenly favors. Awaken in me such confidence in You that their fullness may descend ever more fruitfully upon my soul. I thank You for offering Yourself in thanksgiving to God for all His benefits, spiritual and temporal, which He has bestowed upon me.

In union with Your offering of Yourself to Your Father in the Holy Sacrifice of the Mass, I ask for this special favor: *(Mention your request).*

If it be Your holy Will, grant my request. Through You I also hope to receive the grace of perseverance in Your love and faithful service, a holy death, and a happy eternity with You in heaven. Amen.

Prayer to Christ the High Priest

L ORD Jesus Christ, our great High Priest, by Your Death and Resurrection You revealed Yourself as the mediating Lamb of Sacrifice between the Father and ourselves. You call us to share Your dying and rising in the Sacraments of Baptism and Confirmation so that we might unite ourselves in offering Your sacrifice through Your Priesthood in the Eucharist, thus entering into Your Kingdom on earth by becoming Your Holy People.

Lord Jesus Christ, our great High Priest, grant to us Your Spirit of Love and Life which unites us to Yourself as Victim and Priest so that God's plan of salvation for all people is established within us.

Lord Jesus Christ, our great High Priest, grant to us Your Spirit of Wisdom and Unity which makes us all one in Your Mystical Body, the Church, so that we may be Your witnesses in this world.

Lord Jesus Christ, our great High Priest, heal us by Your Cross, renew us by Your Resurrection, sanctify us by Your Holy Spirit, glorify us by Your Kingship, redeem us by Your Priesthood, so that we may be one in You as You are one with Your Father in the Holy Spirit.

Lord Jesus, gather us all into Your Person—Victim, Priest, King—by the saving Eucharistic Meal You and we offer on the Altar of Sacrifice now and all of our pilgrim days on earth. Then when we are called into Your Kingdom in heaven, may we share with all the Saints the glory of Your love and life which is Yours with the Father and the Holy Spirit for all ages to come without end. Amen.

Prayer

O LORD, You have given us this Sacred Banquet, in which Christ is received, the memory of His Passion is renewed, the mind is filled with grace, and a pledge of future glory is given to us.

℣. You have given them bread from heaven.

℟. *Containing in itself all sweetness.*

LET us pray. God our Father, for Your glory and our salvation You appointed Jesus Christ eternal High Priest. May the people He gained for You by His Blood come to share in the power of His Cross and Resurrection by celebrating His Memorial in this Eucharist, for He lives and reigns with You and the Holy Spirit, one God, forever. ℟. Amen.

O Jesus,
in this wonderful Sacrament
You left us a memorial of Your Passion.
Grant us so to venerate the sacred mysteries
of Your Body and Blood
that we may ever continue to feel within us
the fruit of Your Redemption.
You live and reign forever and ever.
℟. Amen.

NOVENA
OF HOLY COMMUNIONS

MEDITATION

THE Sacrifice of the Mass is not only a ritual which reminds us of the sacrifice of Calvary. In it, through the ministry of priests, Christ continues till the end of time the Sacrifice of the Cross in an unbloody manner. The Eucharist is also a meal which reminds us of the Last Supper, celebrates our unity together in Christ, and already now makes present the Messianic banquet of the Kingdom of Heaven.

Jesus nourishes our soul with Himself, the Bread of Life. He offered Himself as a sacrifice on the Cross. In Holy Communion we partake of the Body that was given in death for us and the Blood that was shed for our salvation. This holy meal reminds us of what happened at the Last Supper when Jesus told His Apostles to do this in memory of Him.

The Communion of the Mass is the meal of the Lord's Body that nourishes us with the life of God and unites us to Jesus and to one another. In drawing us to union with Jesus, our heavenly Father draws us closer to each other because we share in the Divine life of Jesus through His grace. The Holy Eucharist is not only a sign of the unity and love that binds us to Jesus and each other, but it gives us the grace we need to make that love strong and sincere.

Holy Communion is already giving us a part of the banquet of Christ in the Kingdom of Heaven because it is the same Son of God made Man Who will be united with us in a union of joy forever in heaven. Jesus also promised that our body would some day enjoy His presence. He said, "Whoever eats My Flesh and drinks My Blood has eternal life, and I will raise him up on the last day" (Jn 6:54). The meal, prepared for us by God the Father, prepares us to take part in that heavenly communion with Jesus and His Father.

In the Eucharist Jesus nourishes Christians with His own Self, the Bread of Life, so that they may become a people more pleasing to God and filled with greater love of God and neighbor.

Holy Communion is Jesus Christ Himself under the appearances of bread and wine uniting Himself to the Christian to nourish his soul. He said, "I am the living Bread That came down from heaven. Whoever eats this Bread will live forever; and the bread that I will give is My Flesh, for the life of the world" (Jn 6:51).

Holy Communion helps us to love God more because of the Divine grace which grows in our souls. This same grace helps us to love others for the love of God. Jesus strengthens us through actual or sacramental grace that we may overcome temptation and avoid sinning against God and our neighbor. Only by the help of His grace can we truly live a life of charity and fulfill His greatest commandment.

Therefore, the Eucharist is a Sacrament of unity because it unites the faithful more closely with God and with one another. By eating the Body of the Lord, we are taken up into a close union with Him and one another. St. Paul said, "Because there is one loaf of Bread we who are many are one body, for we all partake of the one loaf" (1 Cor 10:17).

The following suggestions about the Novena of Holy Communions may be useful: (1) Receive Holy Communion nine days in succession or on nine Sundays in petition for a special favor. Omitting one or more days of the Novena in no way affects the fruitfulness of the Novena. The power of the Novena is based on our Lord's words: "If you abide in Me and My words abide in you, you may ask for whatever you wish, and it will be done for you" (Jn 15:7). "Whoever eats My Flesh and drinks My Blood dwells in Me, and I dwell in him" (Jn 6:56).

(2) After you have made your novena of *petition* for a special favor, make another immediately in *thanksgiving,* even if you have not received the favor you prayed for. The Novena of Holy Communions is meant to be like a perpetual novena. It is a sacramental novena. The Eucharist is the richest source of grace, and the Mass is the highest form of worship.

Your prayers at Holy Communion were answered—perhaps not in your way, but in God's way; and He knows best! You have done our Lord's Will, for He said at the Last Supper, "Take this and eat; this is My Body. . . . Drink from this, all of you. For this is My Blood of the Covenant, which will be shed on behalf of many for the forgiveness of sins" (Mt 26:26-27). You have also fulfilled the wish of the Church.

SHORT FORM

THE WORD OF GOD

"I am the Vine, you are the branches. Whoever abides in Me, and I in him, will bear much fruit. Apart from Me you can do nothing." —Jn 15:5

"Amen, amen, I say to you, unless you eat the Flesh of the Son of Man and drink His Blood, you do not have life in you." —Jn 6:53

"Now it is no longer I who live, but it is Christ Who lives in me. The life I live now in the body I live by faith in the Son of God Who loved me and gave Himself up for me." —Gal 2:20

"Where your treasure is, there will your heart also be." —Lk 12:34

NOVENA PRAYERS

Novena Prayer

JESUS, my Eucharistic Friend, accept this Novena of Holy Communions which I am making in order to draw closer to Your Sacred Heart in sincerest love. If it be Your holy Will, grant the special favor for which I am making this novena: *(Mention your request).*

Jesus, You have said, "Ask and you shall receive; seek and you shall find; knock and it shall be opened to you" (Mt 7:7). Through the intercession of Your most holy Mother, Our Lady of the Blessed Sacrament, I ask, I seek, I knock; please grant my prayer.

Jesus, You have said, "If you ask the Father for anything in My Name, He will give it to you" (Jn 16:23). Through the intercession of Your most holy Mother, Our Lady of the Blessed Sacrament, I ask the Father in Your Name to grant my prayer.

Jesus, You have said, "Whatever you ask in My Name I will do" (Jn 14:13). Through the intercession of Your most holy Mother, Our Lady of the Blessed Sacrament, I ask in Your Name to grant my prayer.

Jesus, You have said, "If you abide in Me, and My words abide in you, you may ask for whatever you wish, and it will be done for you" (Jn 15:7). Through the intercession of Your most holy Mother, Our Lady of the Blessed Sacrament, may my request be granted, for I wish to live in You through frequent Holy Communion.

Lord, I believe that I can do nothing better in order to obtain the favor I desire than to attend Holy Mass and to unite myself in Holy Communion most intimately with You, the Source of all graces. When You are really and truly present in my soul as God and Man, my confidence is greatest, for You want to help me, because You are all-good; You know how to help me, because You are all-wise; You can help me, because You are all-powerful. Most Sacred Heart of Jesus, I believe in Your love for me!

Jesus, as a proof of my sincerest gratitude, I promise to receive You in Holy Communion as often as I am able to do so—at every Mass I attend, if possible. Help me to love You in the Holy Eucharist as my greatest Treasure upon earth. May the effects of frequent Holy Communion help me to serve You faithfully so that I may save my soul and be with You forever in heaven. Amen.

Hymn—Adoro Te

HIDDEN God, devoutly I adore You,
Truly present underneath these veils:
All my heart subdues itself before You,
Since it all before You faints and fails.

Not to sight, or taste, or touch be credit,
Hearing only do we trust secure;
I believe, for God the Son has said it—
Word of Truth that ever shall endure.

On the cross was veiled Your Godhead's splendor,
Here Your Manhood lies hidden too;
Unto both alike my faith I render,
And, as sued the contrite thief, I sue.

Though I look not on Your wounds with Thomas,
You, my Lord, and You, my God, I call:
Make me more and more believe Your promise,
Hope in You, and love You over all.

O memorial of my Savior dying,
Living Bread, that gives life to man;
Make my soul, its life from You supplying,
Taste Your sweetness, as on earth it can.

Deign, O Jesus, Pelican of heaven,
Me, a sinner, in Your Blood to lave,
To a single drop of which is given
All the world from all its sin to save.

Contemplating, Lord, Your hidden presence,
Grant me what I thirst for and implore,
In the revelation of Your essence
To behold Your glory evermore.

Saint Thomas Aquinas

For Frequent Communicants

LOVING Jesus, You came into the world to give to all souls Your Divine life. To preserve and strengthen this supernatural life and to sustain us against our daily weaknesses and shortcomings, You wished to become our daily Food.

Humbly we beg You, pour forth Your Divine Spirit upon us through the love of Your Sacred Heart. May the souls who, through the misfortune of sin, have lost the life of grace, return once more to You.

Let those who share Your Divine life come to Your Holy Table frequently, that by partaking of this Holy Banquet, they may receive the strength to be victorious in the daily struggle with sin and thus grow ever purer and holier in Your sight, till they come to eternal life with You. Amen.

Our Lady of the Blessed Sacrament

VIRGIN Mary, Our Lady of the most Blessed Sacrament, glory of the Christian people, joy of the Universal Church, salvation of the whole world, pray for us and grant to all the faithful true devotion to the most Holy Eucharist, that they may become worthy to receive it daily.

Prayer

SACRED Banquet, in which Christ is received, the memory of His Passion is renewed, the mind is filled with grace, and a pledge of future glory is given to us.

℣. You have given them bread from heaven.

℟. *Containing in itself all sweetness.*

LET us pray.
O God,
in this wonderful Sacrament
You left us a memorial of Your Passion.
Grant us, so to venerate the sacred mysteries
of Your Body and Blood
that we may ever continue to feel within us
the fruit of Your Redemption.
You live and reign forever and ever. ℟. Amen.

NOVENA
OF HOLY COMMUNIONS

LONG FORM

FIRST DAY

Christ-Likeness

*T*HE *greatest blessing that Holy Communion gives me is an increase of sanctifying grace, the very life of my soul.* It makes me share in Your own divine life. "Whoever eats My Flesh, and drinks My Blood dwells in Me and I dwell in him" (Jn 6:56). Just as the heavenly Father gives You His Divinity, His power, His goodness, His life, from all eternity, so do You give me Your divine life in Holy Communion. "Just as I have life because of the Father, so whoever eats Me will also live because of Me" (Jn 6:57).

As the stem and the branches of a vine are one same being, nourished and acting together, producing the same fruits because they are fed by the same sap, so, too, You circulate Your divine life of grace in my soul through Holy Communion in such a way that I live by Your life and really become Christlike. "Just as a branch cannot bear fruit by itself unless it remains attached to the vine, so you cannot bear fruit unless you abide in Me. I am the Vine, you are the branches. Whoever abides in Me, and I in him, will bear much fruit. Apart from Me you can do nothing" (Jn 15:4-6).

How marvelous is the fruit of sanctifying grace! It makes my soul holy, beautiful and pleasing to God, a sacred temple of the Holy Spirit. Sanctifying grace, which is increased in my soul in Holy Communion, not only makes me an adopted child of God but also helps me to act as another Christ. It gives me the right to enter heaven, for without grace I can never see God.

People try to be great and attractive in the eyes of the world. They seek riches, honor, and beauty; but I know, dear Jesus, that there is nothing on earth that equals the riches of the sanctifying grace contained in one Holy Communion; that there is nothing more beautiful than a soul adorned with grace. The more grace I have, the holier and happier I shall be in time and in eternity, for by grace I know You more clearly, I love You more sincerely, and I possess You more securely. How precious is this union between my soul and You, my God and my All! This union is made possible by the love of Your Sacred Heart and is effected by the grace I receive at Holy Communion.

Lord Jesus, help me to appreciate sanctifying grace. May it mean more to me than everything else on earth. And since it is my treasure, may my heart be ever set upon it in conformity with Your words, "Where your treasure is, there will your heart also be" (Lk 12:34). Let me hate and shun whatever may put me in danger of losing sanctifying grace through mortal sin.

Jesus, I believe You make me Christlike not only by giving me sanctifying grace in Holy Communion but also by giving me actual graces— helps from above—to preserve Your divine life in my soul. Through these helps given me in Holy Communion and in time of need, my mind receives the light to see and my will is imbued with the strength to do what is right and avoid what is wrong. Through frequent Holy Communion, help me to think and desire, speak and act like You. Make my thoughts upright, my desires pure, my words kind, my actions holy.

As You are the Image of the Eternal Father, let me try to be as closely as possible the image of You. Detach my heart from myself and from everything created, so that I may give myself to You with my whole heart as You give Yourself to me. In this sacred union may Your love and mine, Your thought and mine, become one for the glory of God and the salvation of my soul. May Your Spirit rule me so completely that You alone may be the aim and the ideal of my life, and that like St. Paul I may exclaim, "Now it is no longer I who live, but it is Christ Who lives in me" (Gal 2:20).

Novena prayer, p. 24.

SECOND DAY

Mary-Likeness

HOLY Communion makes me both Christ-like and Marylike. Only when I become like You and Mary— completely dependent on God's holy Will and His love—only then shall I possess the land of eternal bliss beyond the grave.

Jesus in the Sacrament of the Altar, You are the one Source of my holiness; therefore, my aim should be to reach You. I am holy only insofar as I become like You and belong to You through perfect love. Of myself I am poor and helpless. For this reason You have given me, in Your last moments on the Cross, Your own dear Mother so that she might be my very own. "Woman, behold your son. . . . Behold your Mother" (Jn 19:27).

No one ever belonged to You so completely as did Your Mother. You spent the greater part of Your life on earth in her company, but You lived in her by Your love and grace more intimately than You do in all the Angels and Saints. I wish to imitate Your example; I wish to belong entirely to Your dear Mother, for this is Your Will. *I give everything I have to Mary in order that I may, in as nearly perfect a manner as possible, give all to You for Your greatest glory through the hands of Your own Mother.*

You willed to make Your Mother a perfect image of Yourself. She is the masterpiece of God's creation. She is so much like You that You want me to love her, and by loving and honoring her to become more like her—Marylike. Only then shall I be truly Christlike.

Jesus, I wish to imitate Your Mother especially in her devotion to You in the Blessed Sacrament of the Altar. It was the summary of her last years on earth. How fervently she united herself with You as St. John daily offered the holy Sacrifice of the Mass in his own home. She saw the Sacrifice of Calvary repeated before her very eyes, though now in an unbloody manner. With what ardent love she received You into her heart daily in Holy Communion! It was the same Body she had conceived by the Holy Spirit at the Annunciation, the infant Body she had carried in her arms at Bethlehem, the bleeding Body she had seen hanging in torments upon the Cross on Calvary, the glorified Body which had ascended into heaven.

What emotion she must have felt as she recalled before the Eucharist all those happy and sorrowful events of her life with You! Her faith and love pierced the thin veil which separated her from You. Help me to love and imitate her as Our Lady of the Blessed Sacrament, because she gave You to me. From her, the most pure Virgin, You assumed flesh and blood so that You might redeem me and become the Food of my soul in Holy Communion.

Jesus, at Holy Communion I become Your sanctuary, but what a poor dwelling I offer You, the King of heaven and earth! May You ever find Mother Mary in my heart when I receive You! She will entertain You within me and offer her

Immaculate Heart to be Your dwelling place because You find Your delight wherever she is. Do not behold my poor soul, but rather look upon the virtues and merits of Your dear Mother to whom I belong.

Jesus, I realize that I cannot be a true child of Mary, nor can I be like Mary unless I have a very tender devotion to You in the Sacrament of the Altar. The Holy Eucharist must be my treasure as it was hers. I can do nothing that would please You or her more than to be Marylike in my devotion to the Holy Eucharist. Mary is the shortest and surest and easiest way to Your Eucharistic Heart. May frequent Holy Communion make me Marylike in order that I may become more Christlike!

Novena prayer, p. 24.

THIRD DAY

Joyfulness

L ORD, *I believe that Holy Communion is the surest way to true joy, because It unites me in divine love with You, my greatest and most lovable God.* True joy springs from divine love. How earnestly You invite me to this Banquet of divine love which You prepared for my soul so that I might partake of Your own Body and Blood! "Come to Me, all you who are weary and overburdened, and I will give you rest" (Mt 11:28). As bread imparts to the body strength and a feeling of contentment, so does the Bread of

Life bring peace and joy to my heart because of the wonderful fruits of grace which It produces in my soul. At Holy Communion there is opened to me a world of life, light, and love, a gracious outpouring of the treasures of Your Sacred Heart.

Jesus, the moments of union with You in Holy Communion are the happiest of my life. How much this union of love means to me! It is the climax of Your divine love for me and it should therefore be the object of my fondest desires. You have made my heart for Yourself. It yearns to be with You and to possess You even here on earth so that it may prepare itself for an eternal union with You in heaven. At Holy Communion I enjoy a foretaste of heaven, for I receive Your glorified Body and Blood, Your Soul and Divinity.

Jesus, You have encouraged me to pray for this spiritual joy. "Ask and you will receive, so that your joy may be complete" (Jn 16:24). I pray for the grace to love Holy Communion as the source of true happiness. May Your words to the Apostles be fulfilled in me through Holy Communion: "You are now in anguish, but I will see you again, and your hearts will rejoice, and no one shall deprive you of your joy" (Jn 16:22).

In Holy Communion let me see You frequently with eyes of faith, so that my heart may rejoice. This is the true and lasting joy which neither the world nor the powers of evil can take from me. May Your true joy overflow into my heart—joy that will make me forget the storms and trials of life and the fleeting pleasures of time.

Jesus, make me resolve to tread under foot all that is low and earthly so that I may strive to find my rest in You alone. Preserve my soul from sin. It is the cause of all unhappiness in this world, since it deprives souls of Your friendship. *May frequent Holy Communion fill my heart with joyfulness that will make serving You a pleasure even in the midst of the greatest sacrifices.*

Holy Communion fills my heart with joy because It fills my soul with many graces which are the source of true joy. At this Fount of joy I find the strength and courage to undertake great things for Your glory and the welfare of my neighbor. Holy Communion is the foundation of my faith, the support of my hope, the nourishment of my charity, for It inflames my heart with Your love. It is the most efficacious means I have of sanctifying and saving my soul.

My heart is filled with bliss because You make it Your little heaven of delights when You visit me in Communion. With Your dear Mother I thank You for this great Treasure: "My soul proclaims the greatness of the Lord, and my spirit rejoices in God my Savior . . . because He Who is mighty has done great things for me" (Lk 1:47-49).

Novena prayer, p. 24.

FOURTH DAY

Prayerfulness

L ORD, You gave me prayer as an unfailing means of salvation and holiness, and You *promised that my prayers would be heard.* "Ask, and it will be given you; seek, and you will find; knock, and the door will be opened to you. For everyone who asks will receive, and those who seek will find; and to those who knock, the door will be opened" (Mt 7:7-9). "Whatever you ask for in prayer, believe that you have received it, and it will be yours" (Mk 11:24). But this will happen on *the condition that I abide in You,* for You also said, "If you abide in Me, and My words abide in you, you may ask for whatever you wish and it will be done for you" (Jn 15:7).

"Abide in Me, and I in you" was Your farewell appeal for my love the night before You died. You told me why I should be united with You by love. "Just as a branch cannot bear fruit by itself unless it remains attached to the vine, so you cannot bear fruit unless you abide in Me" (Jn 15:4). I can do nothing without You; I can obtain nothing without You. I need Your help and Your grace. Let me abide in You and do You abide in me, that my prayers may be heard.

Jesus, You tell me that it is through love that we abide in each other. "As the Father has loved Me, so have I loved you. Remain in My love" (Jn 15:9). In no other way can I be more intimately united with You in divine love than by the Sacrament of Your love. You said, "Whoever eats My Flesh, and drinks My Blood, dwells in Me and I in him" (Jn 6:56). Give me the grace to receive You in Holy Communion often so that my love for You may grow ever more fervent and my prayers may become more powerful.

Lord, I believe that *the special effect of Holy Communion is that It makes me grow in my love for You* by giving me an increase of sanctifying grace. Through love, You take possession of my whole being. Your first and greatest commandment is that I love You with my whole heart and above all things.

Through Holy Communion help me to love You with my whole *heart*—with undivided love, so that I may love nothing created except for Your sake. Whatever is not loved and sought for Your sake is worthless and only burdens the soul.

Through Holy Communion help me to love You with my whole *soul*—with all my inclinations. You are always the same and with utmost confidence I can rely wholly on You. Make me hate sin above every other evil, for only then will my soul be well disposed and blessed with Your peace.

Through Holy Communion help me to love You with my whole *mind*—so that I may value Your good pleasure, Your grace, Your heaven, above everything else, above my convenience, above all earthly treasures, above all knowledge and friendship, above health and life.

Through Holy Communion help me to love You with all my *strength*— so that my eyes, ears, tongue, hands, and feet, my imagination, memory, understanding, and will may be consecrated to You and Your service. How wretched would I be if, possessing all these faculties of soul and body by the goodness of God, I should misuse them to offend You.

Lord Jesus, the Eucharist is the most wonderful work of Your love. Out of infinite love You have given me not only what You have but what You are. In Holy Communion You give me Your Body, Your Blood, Your Soul, Your Divinity, Your merits, and Your graces. Nowhere do You bestow these graces more abundantly than in this Sacrament. May such love awaken a return of love in my heart! I want to receive You in Holy Communion more frequently so that I may abide in You and You in me. Then will my prayers be truly powerful, because they will come from a heart that is one with Your own in deepest love and friendship. I shall pray to the Father in Your Name and I shall be heard, for You said, "If you ask the Father for anything in My Name, He will give it to you" (Jn 16:23).

Jesus, I can do nothing better than to present my prayers to You after Holy Communion. These moments are most precious, because then You are with me as God and Man for the very purpose of helping me and making me holy. You have promised to hear my prayer, "If you ask Me for anything in My Name, I will do it" (Jn 14:14). You come to my soul to apply to me the merits of Your most holy life, of Your painful sufferings, of Your most bitter Death. You come to enrich me with Your heavenly treasures, to make my body pure and my soul holy, to help me live a life more like Your own. May frequent Communion teach me prayerfulness and make me less unworthy of receiving the favors I ask. Your words give me great confidence: "If you abide in Me and My words abide in you, you may ask for whatever you wish and it will be done for you" (Jn 15:7).

Novena prayer, p. 24.

FIFTH DAY

Kindness

JESUS, when You were about to depart from this world, You laid upon us Your last commendation that we should love one another. "This is My commandment: love one another as I have loved you" (Jn 15:12). You loved me even unto death: "No one can have greater love than to lay down his life for his friends" (Jn 15:13). I must imitate Your example by loving my neighbor with a supernatural love and being kind toward him, for You said, "This is how everyone will know that you are My disciples: your love for one another" (Jn 13:35).

Jesus, I believe that Holy Communion preserves and increases this love for my neighbor. It is a Banquet of Love which You have prepared for the children of God. Even the outward tokens of the Eucharist remind me of brotherly love and kindness. Many grains of wheat are ground and mingled together to make one host, and many grapes are crushed to fill the Eucharistic chalice; similarly must we become one through love and Holy Communion. The Eucharist is the bond of charity that unites all Christians as members of one spiritual body, the Church, even as the soul gives life to each member of the human body. Your Apostle says, "The Bread that we break, is it not a sharing in the Body of Christ? Because there is one loaf of Bread, we who are many are one Body, for we all partake of the one loaf" (1 Cor 10:16-17). Jesus, You are that Bread in Holy Communion.

Through frequent Holy Communion help me to carry out Your great commandment of love for my neighbor and give me the grace to put away all unkindness. I want to love my neighbor as myself for Your sake. Let me respect and love him as God's image and likeness, as a child of our heavenly Father, as the temple of the Holy Spirit. You love him as You love me, and You give Yourself to him in Holy Communion as You give Yourself to me. In fact, You identify Yourself with him, for You said, "Whatever you did for one of the least of these brethren of Mine, you did for Me" (Mt 25:40). How can I disrespect one whom You respect so highly? How can I be unkind to one for whom You offered Your life on the Cross?

Let me be kind to my neighbor as I would have him be kind to me. "In everything, deal with others as you would like them to deal with you" (Mt 7:12). I cannot receive You into a heart that refuses to forgive. This would make me undeserving of Your mercy, for You said, "Forgive, and you will be forgiven. Give and gifts will be given to you" (Lk 6:37).

Lord Jesus, give me the grace to partake of this Banquet of Love frequently so that the merciful love of Your own Heart may be enkindled in mine. I have been nourished with the Flesh and Blood of Christ, the meek Lamb of God, Who "when He was abused did not retaliate" (1 Pet 2:23). Let me never be carried away by anger or by any other passion. *Through frequent Holy Communion give me the pure love for God and neighbor that fills Your own Heart.*

I cannot love God truly unless I also love my neighbor, nor can I love my neighbor as I ought unless I truly love God. Increase both loves in my heart through Holy Communion. May that divine charity be poured out upon Your holy Church through the Sacrament of Your Love so that Your prayer at the Last Supper may be fulfilled: "That they may be one, as We are one, I in them and You in Me, that they may become completely one" (Jn 17:22, 23).

Novena prayer, p. 24.

SIXTH DAY

Sinlessness

L ORD, *I believe that mortal sin is the greatest evil in the world* because it turns me away from God—the Source of all life, peace, and joy. It causes spiritual death. Through it the devil can destroy Your work of grace in my soul.

My life is a continual warfare against the world, the flesh, and the devil—those enemies of my soul that lead me into mortal sin—but You have given me Holy Communion as the most powerful safeguard against them. You teach me that *the main effect of Holy Communion is to preserve and increase the life of sanctifying grace in my soul and to guard it against mortal sin.* "This is the Bread that comes down from heaven, so that one may eat It and not die" (Jn 6:50). *Holy Communion also imparts actual graces which give light and strength*—light to my mind that I may see the evil which I must shun, and strength to my will that I may fight against it.

The Sacred Body which was born of the Virgin Mary sanctifies me and in the time of temptation It helps me to keep my passions under control. The Blood which washes away the sins of the world is my refreshment. By Its divine power I am protected from mortal sin. Everything that surrounds this Sacrament is clean, white, and spotless—reminding me that I must war against all sin and impurity.

Jesus, when I receive You into my heart, I become like a tabernacle which contains the Blessed Sacrament. How chaste my body should be! How can I defile my soul with impure thoughts and desires, much less with sinful actions? Make my words and conversations clean, kind, and proper, for my tongue touches Your most pure Body and serves as a paten on which You rest. I beg You to remain close to me when I am tempted; do not permit any serious sin ever to separate me from You. Do not permit me to commit even lesser sins which would weaken our friendship. Strengthen my soul by the power of Your grace, that I may courageously resist all evil. I should fear nothing, for I am equipped with the strongest spiritual weapon—Holy Communion. If You are with me, who can be against me?

Jesus, I believe that after mortal sin nothing is more terrible than venial sin. It really offends Your infinite majesty and brings upon me the punishments of purgatory. It banishes true joy from my heart because it draws me away from You, my highest Good. Venial sin is an ugly stain which makes my soul displeasing in Your sight. It hinders You from enriching me with so many more graces which could help me to love and serve You better.

I thank You for Holy Communion, which prevents mortal sin from taking root in my soul and washes away the stains of venial sin so long as I have no affection for it or desire to commit it in the future. Your coming to me awakens new love in my heart and encourages me to live in purity and sinlessness for Your glory alone.

Sinlessness is a reflection of Your own divine beauty. It draws Your Heart in loving friendship. "He that loves cleanness of heart . . . shall have the King for his friend" (Prov 22:11). One Holy Communion should be enough to make my soul holy and sinless, and yet, after so many Communions, I have not succeeded in correcting my faults. It is because I have not received Holy Communion with greater fervor and more often, though You assure me that I cannot keep my soul alive—free from mortal sin—without Holy Communion. "Unless you eat the Flesh of the Son of Man and drink His Blood, you do not have life within you" (Jn 6:53).

Help me to receive Your Sacred Flesh and Blood in Holy Communion often—at every Holy Mass I attend, if possible—so that my soul may be sinless. With the poor leper I cry out to you, "Lord, if You choose to do so, You can make me clean." Stretch forth Your hand and touch me also in Holy Communion and say, "I do choose. Be made clean" (Mt 8:2, 3).

Jesus, I beg You to *cleanse and sanctify my body,* which is privileged to enshrine Your own sacred Body in Holy Communion. Make it a fitting ciborium for the Victim-Body which was sacrificed to atone for my sins. *Wash in Your redeeming Blood all the sinfulness of my soul;* make my being beautiful with the sinlessness of the Angels. Give me all the strength I need to guard the purity of my body and soul and grant that my conscience may never be defiled by any evil thought, desire, word, or deed. Let me rather die than offend You by a willful mortal sin.

May each Holy Communion be a pledge of my loyalty to You until I am eternally Your own in Your heavenly kingdom. Lamb of God, You Who take away the sins of the world, have mercy on me! Through Communion make me sinless and pure of heart so that I may see God!

Novena prayer, p. 24.

SEVENTH DAY

Lowliness

*J*ESUS, *You have always been my Model and Teacher of humility.* You set me many an example by word and deed during Your earthly life, and even more do You do so now in Your sacramental life. You said, "Take My yoke upon you and learn from Me, for I am meek and humble of Heart and you will find rest for your souls" (Mt 11:29). *The Eucharist is not only a school of humility but also the channel of graces which enable me to be lowly and peace-loving.*

Jesus, how great is Your humility in this Sacrament. Though You are the Eternal and Almighty God, You have lowered Yourself, taking the form of man for love of me and for the sake of my salvation. Not only have You become my Elder Brother, a fellow-creature, but You have willed to be the very food of my soul in Holy Communion. Once Your human form cloaked Your Divinity, but now the appearances of bread hide even Your Humanity. I can see You only with eyes of faith.

How humbly You obey Your priests! One word from their lips and You come down upon the altar in Holy Mass and renew the Sacrifice of Calvary in an unbloody manner. You permit Your priests to give You as the Bread of Life to those who come to the Holy Table; You do not shrink even from the unworthy. You allow Yourself to be carried wherever Your priests bear

You. Heaven and earth are subject to You, O King of Glory, and yet You lower Yourself before Your sinful creatures, living with them in the Sacred Host—offering Yourself for them, coming to their hearts in Holy Communion.

The great test of humility is the pain of not receiving love for love, and that, too, You bear. In this Sacrament You live entirely for me. Your unbounded love urges the desire to unite Yourself with me in Holy Communion. You long to enrich me with Your blessings and to gladden my soul. And yet what do I give You in return? What do so many of us Catholics do to return love for love? How many of us pay scant attention to Your invitation! How many of us fail to receive You in Holy Communion frequently!

Too often we are cold and ungrateful, unmindful of Your love, half-hearted or even irreverent at Mass and Holy Communion! You patiently bear with this indifference. Despite our ingratitude You continue to grant us countless blessings, and thus teach us the noblest kind of humility: to love even when love is not returned; to embrace even humiliations.

Jesus, behold how I am in need of lowliness! I rely so much upon myself. I freely boast of the little good that is in me as if it were mine by personal merit, whereas whatever good is in me really comes from You. I seek praise for myself, whereas I should refer it to You. My pride leads me into so many daily faults; to sensitiveness, jealousy, rash judgment, uncharitableness and anger. And yet You say, "Blessed are the peace-makers. . . ." (Mt 5:9). You have urged me to come to terms with my neighbor before I come to Your altar with my gift. "Therefore, when offering your gift at the altar, if you should remember that you have treated your brother badly, leave your gift there at the altar and immediately go to be reconciled with your brother. Then return and offer your gift" (Mt 5:23).

I cannot offer You to Your Father in Holy Mass as my greatest gift as long as I refuse to be a peacemaker. I cannot rest my head upon Your Sacred Heart after Holy Communion and at the same time nurture in my bosom feelings of unkindness toward my neighbor or the refusal to forgive him. You have taught me to love even my enemies. "Love your enemies and pray for those who persecute you. This will enable you to be children of your heavenly Father. For He causes His sun to rise on evil people as well as on those who are good, and His rain falls on both the righteous and the wicked" (Mt 5:44,45).

Jesus, I wish to receive Holy Communion often—at every Holy Mass I attend, if possible— so that the power of Your grace may conquer my pride and that because of Your presence I may enjoy Your peace and spread it among others. Only after I have become like a lowly child shall I enter Your kingdom of peace, for You have said, "Unless you change and become like little children, you will never enter the kingdom of heaven. Whoever humbles himself and becomes like this child is the greatest in the kingdom of heaven" (Mt 18:4).

Novena prayer, p. 24.

EIGHTH DAY

Unselfishness

JESUS, You came upon this earth to glorify Your heavenly Father by Your life and especially by Your Death. *I believe that Your Sacrifice of Calvary is renewed each day in an unbloody manner at Holy Mass.* The separate consecration of the bread and wine reminds me of this: "This is My Body, which will be given for you" (Lk 22:19); "This is My Blood . . . which will be shed for many unto the forgiveness of sins" (Mt 26:28). You offer Yourself to Your Father now, though in an unbloody manner, just as You did on the Cross. You offer Yourself in the same spirit of love and resignation to His holy Will, because You are present in the Sacred Host as the Victim of Calvary. That Sacred Host is my food in Holy Communion. It is the sacrificial Banquet which completes the Sacrifice of the Mass.

By Holy Communion I unite myself with You as You offer Yourself again to Your Father, and I become one sacrifice with You, for You have said, "Whoever eats My Flesh and drinks My Blood dwells in Me and I dwell in him" (Jn 6:56). *May Holy Communion give me the true spirit of Christlike unselfishness and sacrifice which I need throughout life in order to follow You!*

O Victim-Savior, *these gifts of bread and wine specifically set aside for God's honor in the Mass symbolize the gift of myself that I make in union with You.* As they belong to God, so may I belong entirely to Him, the Giver and Master of my life, my greatest Good. As they are changed into Your own Body and Blood at the Consecration of Holy Mass, so may I be changed into You by my Holy Communions with You, the Victim of Calvary.

Jesus, I believe that Holy Communion opens the treasury of all the graces which You merited for me by Your bloody Death on the Cross. Oh, may its richest grace be for me a most intimate union with You, so that I may become a living holy victim, pleasing to God, and that all the actions, sufferings, tears, and disappointments of my life may be thus consecrated to You as a sacrifice for the glory of God. Can I live for worldly comforts and pleasures after receiving You as the Victim of Calvary, as One offered, as a slain, sacrificial Lamb of God?

Jesus, Divine Victim of the altar, give my heart sentiments like Your own *so that I may become a worthy co-victim with You through Holy Communion.* I promise to receive You often and fervently, that I may gradually die to my unworthy desires and inclinations, and dedicate myself entirely to Your holy service in the spirit in which You glorified God in life and continue to glorify Him in the Mass. *Give me Your spirit of unselfishness,* for I want to live no more for myself, but for God. As You give Yourself entirely to me, let me give myself entirely to You; in sickness and in health, in failure and in success, in disgrace and in honor, in prosperity and in adversity, in life and in death.

Everything that You send me, or permit in my life, whether favorable or unfavorable, sweet or bitter, is acceptable to me, for I have resolved to conform myself to the divine Will in all things. You invite me to do so: "Take My yoke upon you. . . . For My yoke is easy and My burden is light" (Mt 11:29-30). May God's Will always be my will. Thus may each Holy Mass and Holy Communion make me a living image of You, so that the heavenly Father, looking upon me, a co-victim with You in Holy Communion, may say of me what He said of You, "This is My beloved Son, in Whom I am well pleased" (Mt 17:5).

Novena prayer, p. 24.

NINTH DAY

Eucharist-Mindedness

JESUS, how lovingly You call me closer to Your Sacred Heart in Holy Communion, where alone I can find the rest that my troubled soul needs! And yet instead of being Eucharist-minded, I am so very world-minded. Invariably I take better care of my body than I do of my soul. You warned me against such a mistake: "Do not work for food that perishes but for the food that endures for eternal life, which the Son of Man will give you" (Jn 6:27).

Holy Communion will give my soul life ever-lasting. This is Your promise: "I am the living Bread that came down from heaven. Whoever eats this Bread will live forever; and the Bread that I will give is My Flesh, for the life of the world" (Jn 6:51), "Whoever eats My Flesh and drinks My Blood has eternal life, and I will raise him up on the last day" (Jn 6:54).

Jesus, I believe that it is Your Divine life, given to me at Holy Communion, that will make my soul live forever. That divine life flows into my soul during our union of love in Holy Communion, for You said, "Whoever eats My Flesh and drinks My Blood dwells in Me and I dwell in him. Just as I have life because of the Father so whoever eats Me will live because of Me" (Jn 6:56, 57).

This Divine Bread is the spiritual food of my soul. *As food strengthens my body, Holy Communion nourishes and strengthens my soul by grace.* It gives me the strength I need to overcome all the temptations of the world, the flesh, and the devil. It gives me the help I need to practice virtue.

Since Holy Communion means so much for my soul, I can do nothing better than to receive It frequently. It is Your earnest wish that I do so. For this reason You made Your Apostles priests at the Last Supper and ordered them to offer up Holy Mass in Your Name. Your words, "Take this and eat; this is My Body" (Mt 26:26), were meant for me also. Since I offer the Holy Sacrifice together with the priest, I should also receive Holy Communion as the priest does, for *Holy Communion is the Sacred Banquet to which we are invited for complete participation in this Sacrifice.* You are present in this Sacrament not only to offer Yourself *for* me but also to offer Yourself *to* me, to be the Food of my soul.

Your Holy Church wants me to be Eucharist-minded even as You do. She urges me to receive Your Sacred Body in every Holy Mass I attend, and thus participate most intimately in the Divine Sacrifice. This was the spirit of the first Christians, and Mother Church would have me imitate them. To live of the Eucharist and by the Eucharist was the characteristic note of the early Church. *I, too, wish to be Eucharist-minded and make Holy Mass and Holy Communion my only Treasure in this life.*

Lord Jesus, nowhere is Your love for me greater than in this Sacrament. Your gift of love to me is nothing less than Yourself, whole and entire: Your Body, Blood, Soul, and Divinity. You are generous, not for Your own sake but for the sake of my salvation and happiness. Love for me urged You to leave with me the treasure of Communion as a parting testament the night before You died. I can make no better return of love than to receive You often in this Sacrament of Love.

My unworthiness and sinfulness should not keep me away from Your Holy Table; rather, conscious of my short-comings, I should come to You more frequently in order that my soul may be cleansed and sanctified. Only thus shall I become less unworthy of receiving You. Cure my blindness. Give me the grace to overcome my carelessness and lack of faith.

Jesus, be my Companion through life by frequent Communion; be my unfailing Companion during the last painful struggle of death. Come in that decisive hour to protect my soul which You bought with Your own Precious Blood, and lead me safely into the home of Your Father and mine. Help me to receive each Communion as if It were my last. May It be my great devotion in life and my consolation in the hour of death.

Jesus, I thank You for Your kind invitation: "Come to Me, all you who labor and are overburdened, and I will give you rest" (Mt 11:28). My soul is weary and sad; come in Holy Communion and refresh it. Let my heart rest in You alone. I know that I cannot give You greater pleasure than by opening my heart to You so that You may abide there. You desire it because it is in this way that You can most surely save my soul.

You became Man and died on the Cross to save me. Apply the merits of Your sacred Passion and Death to my poor soul in Holy Mass and Communion. I want to receive You at every Holy Mass I attend, if possible. I pledge myself to receive You as often as I can. From now on I am resolved to be more Eucharist-minded. Oh, please give me that grace, for only then can I really become a Saint!

Novena prayer, p. 24.

PRAYERS BEFORE
THE BLESSED SACRAMENT

MEDITATION

THE Eucharist is reserved in our churches to be a powerful help to prayer and the service of others. Reservation of the Blessed Sacrament means that at the end of Communion the remaining Consecrated Bread is placed in the tabernacle and reverently reserved. The Eucharist reserved is a continuing sign of our Lord's real presence among His people and spiritual food for the sick and dying.

We owe gratitude, adoration, and devotion to the Real Presence of Christ in the Blessed Sacrament reserved. We show this devotion in our visits to the tabernacle in our churches and in Benediction when the Blessed Sacrament is exposed to the people for reverence and adoration and the priest blesses the people with the Lord's Body.

The tombs of the Martyrs, the paintings on the walls in the catacombs, and the custom of reserving the Blessed Sacrament in the homes of the first Christians in the years of persecution show the unity of faith in the first centuries of Christianity in the doctrine that in the

Eucharist Christ is really contained, offered, and received. From the Eucharist the entire Church drew
strength for courageous struggles and brilliant victories.

The Eucharist is the center of all Sacramental life because it is of the greatest importance for uniting and
strengthening the Church.

Act of Desire

JESUS,
   I come to You.
You are the *Way*
that I want to follow
in obedience to Your commandments,
Your counsels, and Your example.
Let me walk after You
in the way of obedience, self-denial, and sacrifice
that leads to heaven and to You.

Jesus,
You are the *Truth*.
You are the true Light that enlightens
everyone who comes into the world.
I believe in You.
I believe in Your Gospel.
I want to know You that I may love You.
I want to make You known
in order to make You loved.

Jesus,
You are the *Life*,
through Your sanctifying grace
that is the life of our souls;
through Your words
that are "the words of everlasting life";
through Your Eucharist

that is "the living Bread that has come down
  from heaven";
through Your Heart
that is the fountain of life
for individual souls and for society.

I cling to Your Word
with all my heart.
I hunger for the living Bread
of Your Eucharist.
I open my heart eagerly to the life-giving streams
from Your Sacred Heart.
I unite myself inwardly to all Its intentions.
May this Divine Heart reign universally
over the children of the Church
and over all humanity.
Amen.

Prayer To Return Christ's Love

MY loving Jesus,
  behold to what lengths
Your boundless love has gone!
From Your own Flesh and Precious Blood,
You have prepared for me
a Divine Table
in order to give Yourself
to me.

What has impelled You
to this excess of love?
Nothing else surely
except Your most loving Heart.

O adorable Heart of my Jesus,
burning furnace of Divine Love,
receive my heart

within Your most sacred Wound,
in order that,
in this school of love,
I may learn to make
a return of love
to the God
Who has given me
such wondrous proofs of His great love.
Amen.

Prayer of Adoration and Petition

I ADORE You,
O Jesus,
true God and true Man,
here present in the Holy Eucharist,
as I humbly kneel before You
and unite myself in spirit
with all the faithful on earth
and all the Saints in heaven.

In heartfelt gratitude for so great a blessing,
I love You,
my Jesus,
with my whole soul,
for You are infinitely perfect
and all worthy of my love.
Give me the grace
nevermore in any way to offend You.

Grant that I may be renewed
by Your Eucharistic presence here on earth
and be found worthy to arrive with Mary
at the enjoyment
of Your eternal and blessed presence in heaven.
Amen.

Prayer of Reparation

WITH the deep and humble feeling
that the Faith inspires in me,
O my God and Savior, Jesus Christ,
true God and true Man,
I love You with all my heart,
and I adore You Who are hidden here.

I do so in reparation
for all the irreverences, profanations, and sacri-
leges
that You receive
in the most august Sacrament of the altar.

I adore You,
O my God,
not so much as You are worthy to be adored,
nor so much as I am bound to do,
but at least as much as I am able.
Would that I could adore You
with the perfect worship
that the Angels in heaven are able to offer You.

O Jesus,
may You be known, adored, loved, and thanked
by all people at every moment
in this most holy and Divine Sacrament.
Amen.

Prayer of Thanksgiving and Petition

WE GIVE You thanks,
O Christ, our God;
in Your goodness
You have given us Your Body in this Sacrament
to enable us to live holy lives.
Through Your grace

keep us pure and without stain.
Remain in us to protect us.
Direct our steps in the way
of Your holy and benevolent Will.

Strengthen our souls
against the seductions of the devil
so that we may heed only Your voice
and follow You alone,
O omnipotent and truthful Shepherd,
and attain the place prepared for us
in the Kingdom of Heaven:
O our God and Lord,
Redeemer Jesus Christ,
Who are blessed
with the Father and the Spirit
now and forever.
Amen.

Prayer for Today's Needs

LORD, for tomorrow and its needs I do not
pray;
keep me, my God, from stain of sin, just for today.
Let me both diligently work and duly pray;
let me be kind in word and deed, just for today.
Let me be slow to do my will, prompt to obey;
help me to mortify my flesh, just for today.
Let me no wrong or idle word unthinking say;
set a seal upon my lips, just for today.
Let me in season, Lord, be grave, in season gay;
let me be faithful to Your grace, just for today.
And if today my tide of life should ebb away,
give me Your Sacraments Divine, sweet Lord,
today.

So for tomorrow and its needs, I do not pray;
but keep me, guide me, love me, Lord, just for
today.   Sister M. Xavier, S.N.D.

Prayer To Bring Christ into Our Day

L ORD Jesus,
    present before me in the Blessed Sacrament
of the altar,
help me to cast out from my mind
all thoughts of which You do not approve
and from my heart
all emotions that You do not encourage.

Enable me to spend my entire day
as a coworker with You,
carrying out the tasks that You have entrusted to
     me.
Be with me at every moment of this day:
during the long hours of work,
that I may never tire or slacken from Your ser-
     vice;
during my conversations,
that they may not become for me
occasions for meanness toward others;
during the moments of worry and stress,
that I may remain patient and spiritually calm;
during periods of fatigue and illness,
that I may disregard self and think of others;
during times of temptation,
that I may take refuge in Your grace.

Help me to remain generous and loyal to You
     this day
and so be able to offer it all up to You
with its successes that I have achieved by Your
     help

and its failures that occurred
through my own fault.
Let me come to the wonderful realization
that life is most real
when it is lived with You as the Guest
of my soul.
Amen.

Hymn—Adoro Te

See p. 26.

Litany of the Blessed Sacrament
(For Private Devotion)

L ORD, have mercy.
Christ, have mercy.
Lord, have mercy.
Christ, hear us.
Christ, graciously hear us.
God the Father of heaven,
*have mercy on us.**
God the Son, Redeemer of the world,
God the Holy Spirit,
Holy Trinity, one God,
Living Bread, that came down from heaven,
Hidden God and Savior,
Corn of the elect,
Wine whose fruit are virgins,
Bread of fatness, and royal Dainties,
Perpetual Sacrifice,
Clean Oblation,
Lamb without spot,
Most pure Feast,
Food of Angels,
Hidden Manna,

Memorial of the wonders of God,
Super-substantial Bread,
Word made flesh, dwelling in us,
Sacred Host,
Chalice of benediction,
Mystery of faith,
Most high and adorable Sacrament,
Most holy of all sacrifices,
True Propitiation for the living and the dead,
Heavenly Antidote against the poison of sin,
Most wonderful of all miracles,
Most holy Commemoration of the Passion of Christ,
Gift transcending all fullness,
Special Memorial of Divine love,
Affluence of Divine bounty,
Most august and holy Mystery,

* Have mercy on us *is repeated after each invocation.*

Medicine of immortality,

Tremendous and life-giving Sacrament,

Bread made flesh by the omnipotence of the Word,

Unbloody Sacrifice,

Our Feast at once and our Fellow-guest,

Sweetest Banquet, at which Angels minister,

Sacrament of piety,

Bond of charity,

Priest and Victim,

Spiritual Sweetness tasted in its proper source,

Refreshment of holy souls,

Viaticum of such as die in the Lord,

Pledge of future glory,

Be merciful,

spare us, O Lord.

Be merciful,

graciously hear us, O Lord.

From an unworthy reception of Your Body and Blood,

*O Lord, deliver us.***

From the lust of the flesh,

From the lust of the eyes,

From the pride of life,

From every occasion of sin,

Through the desire, by which You desired to eat this Passover with Your disciples,

Through that profound humility, by which You washed their feet,

Through that ardent charity, by which You instituted this Divine Sacrament,

Through Your Precious Blood, that You have left us on our altars,

Through the Five Wounds of this Your most holy Body, that You received for us,

We sinners,

*we beseech You, hear us.****

That You would preserve and increase our faith, reverence, and devotion toward this admirable Sacrament,

That You would conduct us, through a true confession of our sins, to a frequent reception of the holy Eucharist,

That You would deliver us from all heresy, perfidy, and blindness of heart,

That You would impart to us the precious and heavenly fruits of this most holy Sacrament,

That at the hour of death You would strengthen and defend us by this heavenly Viaticum,

---

** O Lord, deliver us *is repeated after each invocation.*

*** We beseech You, hear us *is repeated after each invocation.*

Son of God,
Lamb of God, You take away the sins of the world;
spare us, O Lord.
Lamb of God, You take away the sins of the world;
graciously hear us, O Lord.

Lamb of God, You take away the sins of the world;
have mercy on us.
Christ, hear us.
Christ, graciously hear us.

℣. You gave them Bread from heaven,
℟. *Containing in Itself all sweetness.*

L ET us pray.
   O God,
in this wonderful Sacrament
You left us a memorial of Your Passion.
Grant us so to venerate the sacred mysteries
of Your Body and Blood
that we may ever continue to feel within us
the blessed fruit of Your Redemption.
You live and reign forever and ever. ℟. Amen.

Invocations to Jesus in the Blessed Sacrament

J ESUS in the Blessed Sacrament,
   have mercy on us.

P RAISE and adoration ever more be given
   to the most Holy Sacrament.

O SACRAMENT most holy,
   O Sacrament Divine!
All praise and all thanksgiving
be every moment Thine!